Country

FLOWER

Style

Creating a Natural Look

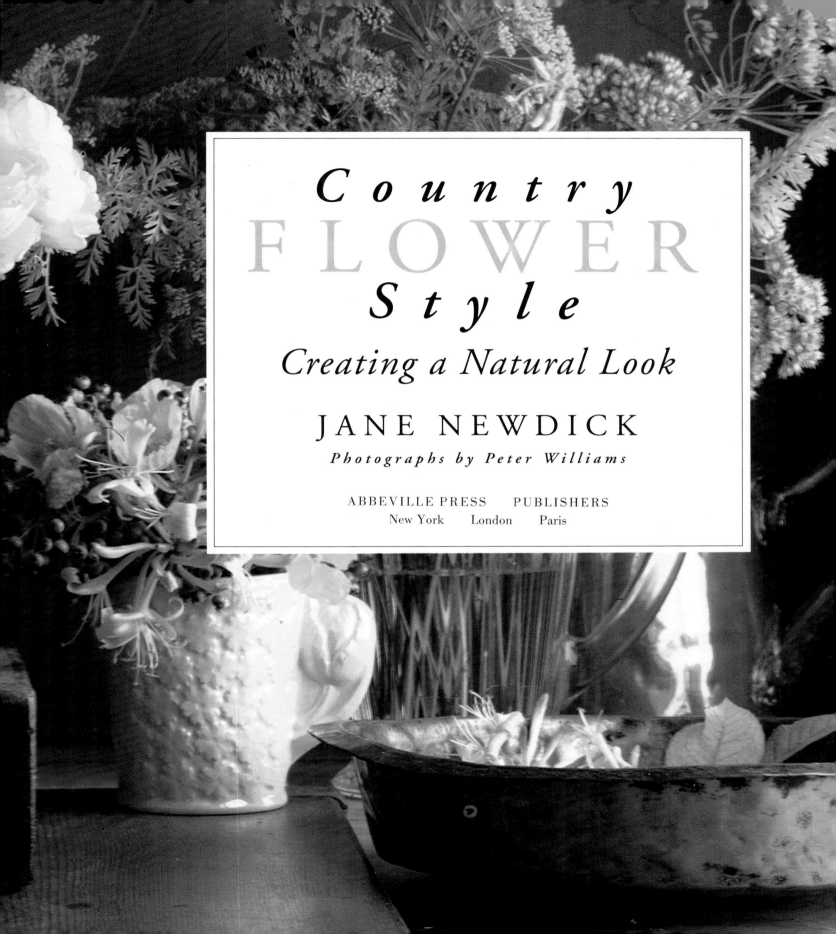

Country FLOWER *Style*

Creating a Natural Look

JANE NEWDICK

Photographs by Peter Williams

ABBEVILLE PRESS   PUBLISHERS
New York   London   Paris

CONTENTS

F lowers in their season displayed as simply as possible is the natural

way to decorate a house. Use their colour, shapes and scents to dictate how

best they will look, and forget artifice and complicated arrangements. Simple

can still mean sophisticated and stylish – it is all to do with approach

and attitude. Just feast your eyes and enjoy the flowers.

Introduction

Defining a Country Style

All flowers have their own innate style. Once you are aware of this, bringing out the best in them is a fairly simple matter. Some flower arranging books suggest you use flowers as areas of colour to be shifted around into some kind of complicated pattern or to fill in a blank canvas like painting by numbers. I can't see them as so much filling-in material but always as individual plants with their own special looks and ways of growing, whether it is in the garden or in immaculate rows in a high tech glasshouse. Every flower has something about it that is worth showing off. It may be its incredibly strong colour, or the special texture of its petals, or maybe the strength and length of its stem or the strange and beautiful outline of its shape. I do believe that you need to spend a little time looking carefully at the materials you have, as this leads to an understanding of the individual character or nature of the flower in front of you.

Growing your own flowers in a garden, however small, is an advantage but not absolutely necessary now that flower shops and market stalls have choices of flowers and foliage only dreamt of fifteen or twenty years ago. People normally choose a bunch of flowers because they like them and the colour is nice and they hope that they will last for a while – all very good reasons for making the choice. Once home, they are gripped by a fear of not knowing what to do next, feeling that they should be following some special ritual to create an arrangement. Don't worry. Do nothing to the flowers except put them in water and enjoy them for the same reasons that you bought them. But if you'd like to move a step or two further on from this stage, then this book will provide you with ideas and inspiration from spring through to winter. In every case the flowers shine through, speaking for themselves and showing off their own inimitable country style.

**RIGHT Terracotta garden pots and elegant
red tulips. Both are lovely things on their own.
Combine them and you have style.**

Finding your Flowers

You are fortunate indeed if you have the kind of garden which can provide things to pick all the year round or have land which can provide wild offerings when they are plentiful. However, buying flowers has never been easier and at last there are all kinds of desirable things being grown and sold – lovely, simple flowers and interesting foliage, berries in season as well as foreign exotics. Country flowers are there alongside the sophisticated blooms, so now the choice is ours. Most flowers from shops will have been conditioned before you buy. This means the stems have been re-cut and given a drink. If you are doubtful or if you buy from a box of flowers on the pavement with no water in sight, cut the stems again (under water if you are really zealous) and stand them in tepid water for a few hours before using. Do use any flower food or conditioner provided with the flowers as it really can improve their keeping qualities.

LEFT Garden flowers have very special, individual
characteristics; there is absolutely nothing mass-produced about them.
ABOVE A mixed hedge provides berries, foliage and seed heads.

The Kitchen Cupboard

Simple flowers need simple containers. Elaborate or fussy vases are intimidating to work with and, in most cases, wrong for the kind of flowers we choose for our homes. Starting off with the right container for the flowers is certainly the single most important factor in making something worth looking at. This is why the first stop for finding suitable things to put the flowers in is the kitchen. Jugs, mugs, bowls and basins have the no-nonsense functional shapes and strong features needed for stylish and confident arrangements so experiment with different pieces of china and crockery. Vases with narrow necks or exaggerated waists can be difficult to use, which is not what you need if you lack confidence in putting flowers together. Plain colours or simple decorations and patterns look good with a maximum number of different flowers and these containers will become the standards in your repertoire, useful over and over again. To add to the collection, buy new and old things when you see them and they appeal to you. The odd chip is irrelevant and can save you a fortune on old pieces. 🍇

LEFT Classic shapes and functional pieces from the kitchen cupboard should form the basis of any flower container collection. The colour and pattern choices will be yours.

13

Clear Choices

Glass containers are versatile and easy. The choice is vast with shapes to suit every kind of flower and generally they are not expensive to buy, unless you go for Lalique or the finest cut crystal. Check around the house to see what glass could be pulled into service as vases.

Every kind of drinking glass from liqueur to tankard could make a home for a small bunch or posy, while jugs and carafes are ideal for larger arrangements. Humble laboratory glasses or measuring phials make unusual and functional containers and a collection of found glass, such as old iridescent sauce bottles or antique ink containers, is perfect for grouping together or for using as specimen jars for single blooms.

One or two much larger simple glass vases are endlessly useful. These might be square or rectangular tanks, straight-sided and stylish, or cylinders both squat and elongated. The simplicity of these shapes means that they will be used time and time again while an elaborate cut glass heirloom might soon become tiresome.

The only drawback to glass, if it should be seen as one, is that stems show through. In most cases this can be a special bonus as you can play with a design by adding stones, pebbles, fruits or twigs below the water line as well as flowers above. For the times when you really do want to hide the inner workings, line the inside of the vase with moss or wrap moss around the outside and wire in place. Pack or wrap soft stems such as grass in a spiral inside the vase for an extra decorative touch, or tuck evergreen leaves which won't deteriorate too quickly under water between flower stems and glass. Keep all glass containers spotlessly clean and sparkling, and change the water frequently when they are filled with flowers to avoid a murky, pond-like look. ❧

RIGHT Everyday glass, clear and coloured, plain and fluted, show just a few of the variety of shapes it is possible to press into service as flower containers.

Wood, Metal, Terracotta

Another good source of containers for filling with flowers is the garden store. Here you may have baskets, wooden trugs or fruit crates, terracotta pots and metal buckets. Don't discard anything which might be suitable just because it wasn't designed for this particular purpose. Think more in terms of whether something is practical, whether it will hold water or floral foam, whether it will stand steadily when filled with flowers and whether it has a good colour or surface texture or interesting and unusual shape.

A basic range of baskets can be the backbone of a good container collection. Choose three or four to cover every type of arrangement, perhaps selecting one miniature basket for tiny blooms or flowering bulbs, two medium-sized baskets (one oblong and one round, with or without a handle), and one large one, low and wide. Terracotta plant pots have become popular to hold cut flowers as well as growing plants. They do look good with certain colours and green foliage but need a waterproof container inside them. Metal containers, such as old galvanized buckets, used tins, even watering cans, are stylish and fashionable, their soft grey finish enhanced by a range of flowers and foliage.

LEFT A treasure trove of good and simple containers made from metal, willow, wood and clay. Search outbuildings and garden sheds for some inspiration and possible trophies.

17

Favourite Things

Everyone has their favourite container for flowers. It may be something passed down through the family which has special meaning and associations or a bargain antique bought from a sale or market stall. It could be a souvenir brought back from a memorable holiday or simply something which got pressed into action as a vase one day and the habit has stuck.

Occasionally it is lovely to use a very delicate or precious piece of china or glass which does not normally get used for flowers. These kinds of things are needed for certain special blooms – the absolutely last or the very first rose of summer, a few stems of lily of the valley from plants which have taken years to flower, or an exquisite and fragile camellia rescued from the rain or biting spring wind. Only something perfectly worthy of it can hold a Valentine posy or a bridal bouquet or a very special bunch someone gave you to say thank you. Traditions build up in this way so that a household may have one particular shallow bowl which always get used to float a magnolia bloom or one single beautiful peony in, or a comfortable pottery jug for all those well-meaning collections of disparate flowers which children love to pick and give, with the stems all different lengths and the slightly wilting flowers definitely not matching.

Using fine bone china or delicate porcelain to put flowers in won't hurt it, but you may find that the water will stain inside a little and any marks will need to be removed with diluted bleach or by scrubbing with a toothbrush and a non-abrasive cleaner. Many containers have awkward nooks and crannies which are difficult to get at and clean really properly, so it is sensible to give them the occasional weak bleach treatment which will also kill any lurking bacteria which could cause flowers to deteriorate more quickly. 🌿

RIGHT An old wooden storage chest holds carefully wrapped pieces of bone china which see the light of day occasionally to show off special flowers or just whenever the mood takes you.

Spring brings the return of light, colour and newness with pastels and sunshine yellows, the brilliance of new foliage and all manner of scents. There are blossoms and bulbs, and plenty of flowers to enjoy again.

THE ARRIVAL OF
Spring

Bursting Buds & Fresh, New Leaves

Spring always holds great promise but it can sometimes dash hopes too. Just when the garden appears to break out into flower and leaf the weather can play cruel tricks and provide a backdrop of icy sleet, freezing winds or simply grey, lacklustre skies. But then suddenly there are a few days of prolonged sun casting high shadows on the first cut of the lawn and with no warning it seems there are dozens of plants in bloom, making brilliant patches of fresh colour where a few days ago there was nothing. In this season it all happens so quickly so catch things while you can.

Most spring bulbs are robust and easy to use as cut flowers, lasting well in water, and as a bonus many of them are scented too. Daffodils and narcissi might seem almost too plentiful to take much notice of but they are the most cheerful and optimistic sort of flowers to use, making sunny pools wherever they stand in the house. It is a pleasure to see the first new foliage appearing as it is sorely missed for arrangements during the autumn and winter. Twigs and stems starting into new leaf or fresh blossom are lovely used alone or mixed with other things.

At this time in the year, there is still
nowhere near the quantity of flowers that there
is later in the summer, but there are at last colour
choices again to be made and new and wonderful
flowers to use. Early spring offers every imaginable
shade of yellow, blue, purple and mauve. There are
whites and creams and later in the season rich sugary
blossom pinks, all off set by translucent vivid greens.
Invariably these strong colours look best used alone or with lots
of different ones mixed together into one great glorious explosion,
though many spring flowers, such as daffodils, are notoriously bad mixers
with other things because of their shape, texture and colour and their
reputation for killing off other flowers they are mixed with. It is possible
to buy a special additive from flower shops or garden centres to put in
the water to counteract this effect. Don't forget, too, all the
smaller spring flowers which are so special – tiny wood violets,
fragile-looking anemones, primroses, scillas and cowslips. These
delicate flowers are all the more precious because they have
survived the snow, wind and rain.

Spring Bulbs

Many spring blooms are from flowering bulbs or corms and the best and most natural way of displaying these is often as they are, growing in soil rather than as cut flowers. A little clump of *anemone blanda*, for example, looks sweet and innocent growing from under a blanket of moss with their ferny leaves and green ruffs, but if picked, they would be lost in anything they were put in or swamped by other larger material mixed with them.

Altogether chunkier flowers such as hyacinths are sold as cut flowers, but again they really do look at their best growing in groups or flowering singly in a bulb glass. Multi flora types, or even better Roman hyacinths (always white), harder to find and beautifully scented, are delicate and lighter than their solid cousins, with airy spaced blooms along each stem and several stems blooming from one bulb. You will probably have to grow these yourself from bulbs planted in the previous autumn though, as they are rarely sold in bloom.

Any small flowering bulbs such as scillas and chinodoxias can be brought indoors for a colourful flowering and then planted out into a garden or container for next year. Lily of the valley roots dug up and gently forced in warmth can be made to flower weeks ahead of the ones left in the garden. The purity and scent of their white bell flowers is magical and their deliciously sweet fragrance will perfume a room. 🌿

LEFT White and blue hyacinths, lily of the valley, anemones, scillas and grape hyacinths show the variety of flowering bulbs and corms. ABOVE A sweetly scented hyacinth grown in a bulb glass.

25

An Unassuming Flower

Violets are the shy and retiring flowers of the plant world. They hide their tiny faces amongst their leaves close to the ground in semi-shady places and bloom in early spring before very much is out. The sweet varieties, scented with their subtle and gentle perfume, have long been grown, or gathered from the wild when there were plenty, to make little bunches or nosegays. They can still sometimes be found for sale, very often tied with matching thin cotton thread and encircled by a few of their own heart-shaped leaves or evergreen ivy. So very unshowy and hardly suitable for large arrangements, one wonders how long they will continue to be seen. They look best arranged into tiny cups or delicate glasses, or standing in a container inside a miniature wicker basket. Violets drink through their leaves and petals so keep them misted with water. To revive a wilting bunch, plunge it under water and keep it there for a few hours to drink deeply.

ABOVE In the Victorian tradition, a buttonhole of scented violets.
RIGHT Put a delicate arrangement of violets and ivy leaves in a stemmed
vase to enjoy privately and personally on a desk or dressing table.

A Spring Window

1

This is an easy way to fill a space with flowers when a slightly formal arrangement is required. Work in situ and line up whole blocks of damp floral foam in plastic trays standing side by side. For this window two blocks of foam are sufficient to fill the space.

2

Work across the foam, putting in branches of conditioned foliage. Young beech leaves, both green and purple, are soft textured with vivid colour and combine with ferns, spurge, rhus and honeysuckle. Shorter stems fall forwards, breaking the edge of the window sill.

3

Once the foliage framework is complete simply add the colour with the flowers. Put the orange ranunculus in place first, evenly spread throughout the arrangement. Then add some deep apricot parrot tulips. These tend to curve downwards and forwards so place near the base and front of the display.

Prima Vera, Primula Veris

Spring has more than its share of yellow flowers. Just think of the wild varieties at this time of year which are yellow – wild narcissi, celandines, primroses, cowslips, dandelions, buttercups and marsh marigolds are just a few. Many of these have a glossy and gilded texture, reflecting the sunshine falling on them which in turn makes them open their petals and face upwards. Perhaps the first flowers of the year are the sweetest, coming at a time when we all crave to see more light and signs of life. Primroses, it seems, are the perfect spring symbol. Pale coloured but bright, soft textured yet tough enough to withstand bad weather, with a fresh scent that is never sickly and an innocent, simple shape like a young child's drawing of a flower.

Never pick them from the wild but grow your own in flower borders or rough grass in the garden. Choose a spot shaded from summer sun and where the roots will always have some moisture as they hate drying out. In the wild, for example, they love the rich, damp conditions of the sides of deep ditches and do not thrive in very light and well drained soils. They will seed and spread themselves for future springs.

Cowslips too will settle in gardens. Their scent is one of the most beautiful of spring and they last very well picked and used indoors as a cut flower. There are plenty of hybrids and garden varieties of primula to choose from as well, many of which are sold in spring as small growing plants, perfect to group together in a basket for an instant splash of sunshine.

LEFT Gold and glossy, a group of spring yellows from buttercups
to Welsh poppies. The colour sings out against a contrasting background.
ABOVE Pale yellow primroses in a sturdy terracotta pot.

Spring Sunshine Yellows

Daffodils and narcissi of all kinds are some of the most obvious flowers of spring. They are bold and blatant and can hardly be ignored. Daffodils usually look their best alone and arranged simply. They do not mix very well with other flowers as they cause them to die more quickly. Think how effective they are growing outdoors in a mass of one colour and type, with only green to offset them, and this will give you the key to using them indoors. Plant groups of miniature daffodil bulbs in pebble, soil or sand-filled glass containers or elegant but rustic stone urns. Support taller narcissi with a network of twigs and fill containers with cut blooms as full as you can for the most splendid and golden effect.

PREVIOUS PAGE A subtle line-up of assorted twigs, just beginning
to reveal the first green leaves and coloured blossoms from their fat buds.
LEFT Contained in black and white, old-fashioned yellow daffodils.
ABOVE Cut stems and growing bulbs make a feast of cheerful blooms.

Talented Tulips

Tulips are enjoying a renaissance as a cut flower now that there are so many good varieties to choose, from the most lean and long-stemmed French tulips to the stocky doubles and flamboyantly fringed parrots. Unjustly seen as a difficult cut flower, you must understand that once in water they continue to grow and curve towards the light. Like so many other flowers, they really do look good in quantity, tightly packed together. This alone means that for many they are a once a year treat given that they are expensive until late in the season. Make things simple by putting tulips into a vase or container which opens out towards the neck and is narrower at the base to fan out the blooms. Invest in growing bulbs like these red tulips or plant some yourself for the most vigorous explosion of flower and put them into a wild container for a dramatic effect.

ABOVE LEFT Small double yellow tulips have lots of pretty foliage.
ABOVE RIGHT Red polka dots and wayward tulips have a fifties feel to them.
RIGHT Leave a vase of glorious yellow and red parrot tulips for a week and they open out and curve gracefully until the first petals drop.

A Cream & White Collection

White and cream colours are not as straightforward as you might think. There are clean whites and milky whites, warm creams and cool greenish creams in flowers, and combining them with a little green foliage for relief makes the most of their subtleties.

The white version of cottage garden honesty makes a very good and little used cut flower. The simple flowers are startlingly pure white and can be used as long-stemmed blooms or cut down into smaller pieces as a filler amongst other bulkier flowers such as tulips and ranunculus. The central basket arrangement here has just a little viburnum foliage at the back to frame the other flowers while a few heavy heads of ranunculus are allowed to drop forward over the edge of the hazel twig basket. This kind of design needs foam as its basis.

Cow parsley is pretty enough to bunch into a container by itself and has no need of any mechanics. Be warned, though, that as it fades the tiny flowers drop everywhere but it is usually worth this irritation to enjoy the filmy but generous effect it gives. The strangely graceful stems of Solomon's seal with their clusters of white and green droplet flowers can be bought from flower shops or picked from the garden. They combine very well with other flowers and are excellent either for large scale arrangements which need great sweeping curves or for standing in a simple narrow container with just one or two other flowers like these delicate aquilegias.

White flowers are very much part of the tradition of spring floral decorations. Churches were decked with starry white woodruff and other 'garnishings' at this time of year, and feast days of Our Lady always used white flowers. We continue to this day and spring brides who have traditional weddings usually carry white bouquets into churches filled with white and cream flowers.

LEFT **Cream and white combined with green can be cool and fresh when using unsophisticated spring flowers in a lavish display. The containers are kept simple too.**

39

Baskets in the Pink

The basket container has become almost a cliché for natural flower arrangements but it is so useful that it still holds an important place. Baskets are good because they are visually unassertive but well textured and coloured and look pleasing with just about any flowers or foliage. Line baskets with dry moss and plastic if you use damp foam inside or arrange flowers into an inner waterproof container, such as a shallow vase or jar. Baskets seem entirely right for arrangements made from a mass or muddle of small scale flowers. Here, thinking pink, there are garden aquilegias with London pride, and pink blossom combined with tulips, primulas and fat, round ranunculus.

LEFT Aquilegia, columbine, Granny's bonnets, call them what you
will, look lovely massed in an old basket mixed with foamy London pride.
ABOVE Victorian baskets filled with ranunculus, tulips and primulas.

Summer arrives on a wave of scented roses and old fashioned flowers. Colours are clean and strong: deep purple, sky blue, sugar pink and vivid red, with pure white as a relief — a profusion of blooms.

THE HEART OF
Summer

Sweet Peas & Perfumed Roses

While this is the time of year when flower arrangers are spoilt for choice with the material they have on offer all around them, paradoxically they are likely to be spending more time outside the house and bothering less with filling vases or making table decorations. In hot weather flowers are sometimes seen as a messy nuisance, dying before they are fully open and filling the house with dropped petals. But the summer can be so short and the choice of flowers so very special that even blooms which only last a day or so can still be hard to resist, especially if they add scent and colour to the whole house.

Summer arrangements need be nothing more than a bunch or posy thrust into the simplest container, with no need for hours spent creating masterpieces with foam and wire unless you have a grand occasion or a summer wedding to decorate for. The first roses and sweet peas entice us to pick them from the garden or flower stall and to mass them into china jugs and homely pottery or loosely arrange them in twiggy baskets or rustic metal buckets. Hedgerows proffer wild flowering grasses and the dullest garden will have something worth picking, even if it is just a range of different foliage in a variety of colours and textures.

Summer flowering shrubs provide many generous blooms
and even a vegetable patch can be a surprising source of
wonderful things to use, such as ferny green carrot
tops or deep bronzy red beetroot leaves. Some
keen gardeners hate having their flowers
picked and their outdoor border displays
spoilt so, if you are one of these, make room some-
where for a patch or row of at least one useful summer cutting
flower such as cornflower, godetia, lavatera or love-in-a-
mist, all easily grown from a packet of seeds. Otherwise
cut carefully from the garden and take only small amounts
of material from any one plant or area and consider
that in many cases you will just be carrying out a
useful spot of summer pruning as well as cheering up
the house. If you are lucky enough to have surplus
summer flowers, air-dry any which are suitable for
this treatment or separate large petals or whole
buds and flower heads and dry these for storing away
to use later in the year. Finally, if the weather is good
enough to eat meals outside, then remember to cut flowers
and use them to decorate the table outdoors too.

A Basket of Garden Roses

Garden roses give the greatest pleasure to pick and arrange as they really do all the work for you. The old fashioned kinds with soft subtle colours always harmonize together without any forethought. Bourbon, Centifolia, Alba, Damask, Moss and Gallica roses offer colours embracing the deepest, duskiest purples and burgundies, and pale pearly pinks and mauves. There are rarely any salmon pinks or orangey shades in the make up of these varieties, but rather a touch of blue, so the pinks and reds always look lovely together. Massing the many petalled heads in a basket makes a dense and deliciously textured arrangement full of perfume and colour. Cut blooms late in the day or very early in the morning. Split the woody stems, then leave them in water for a few hours before arranging.

ABOVE **The densely packed petals of Charles de Mills.**
RIGHT **The small white flowers of the scented Seagull rose contrast
with old fashioned garden roses in maroon and pink.**

Lavender's Blue

Lavender is one of the most popular flower fragrances, evoking times past and yet curiously modern at the same time, but it is not used very much in its own right as a fresh flower in arrangements and decorations. In fact it is more likely to be seen in its dried state in stiff little stooks or filling miniature baskets where the soft velvety purples provide a relief from the stronger reds and golds of many dried flowers. In its fresh form it is gentle and pretty and combines beautifully with other flowers, especially in small mixed bunches of summer garden flowers or used alone in tiny posies. There are many different garden varieties to choose from, some coming into bloom in early summer and others later in the season and continuing to produce the odd bloom or two until the beginning of winter. The most scented types are not always the strongest coloured and these days much of the lavender grown commercially for the dried flower trade is a dwarf type, such as Munstead, with very deep purple flowers. The larger, old fashioned bushy lavenders such as Grappenhall have long-stemmed flowers in a paler mauve with a wonderful fragrance.

Small bunches of different types of lavender picked when the tiny flowers are out at their fullest have been put into a collection of different glass tumblers and stood in an old French glass carrier. Alongside the lavender, a weathered metal bowl has a full blown, scented apricot rose floating in a little water with a pale fresh bud yet to open. All roses look elegant and exotic displayed in this way, demanding that you breath in their scent.

LEFT Fresh lavender sprigs simply displayed in an old French glass carrier beside a subtly coloured rose called Café.
RIGHT A miniature lavender bunch tied with linen thread.

A Garden Wedding

The theme for this rustic garden-held feast is to use the most sumptuous flowers, wines and foods against a backdrop of simple orchard greenery, coarse white hand-woven linen with plain metal, china and glass. The flowers are lavish armfuls of garden lavatera Mont Blanc and white cosmos arranged in galvanized buckets and more delicate, but still informal, bunches of creamy white roses or cloudy white gypsophila in clear glass jars. Finally, tiny metal pails are filled with posies of the palest oyster pink rose buds, sprays of yellow wood strawberries, white sweet peas and a few stronger pink roses to lift the whole display and to relate to other details such as pyramids of blush white peaches and pink satin ribbons jauntily tied to the garden chairs. All these flowers would be easy enough to put together the night before or early on the wedding day.

ABOVE Early evening and the celebrations are about to begin.
RIGHT A romantic mixture of palest roses, sweet peas and tiny woodland
strawberries lit by candles and a scattering of nightlights.

A Border in a Basket

The summer garden and flower shop offer such an abundance of treasures that at times it seems impossible to make use of such plenty. Try to make at least one large scale, spectacular summer arrangement to enjoy some of the best and most beautiful flowers and use a family event or party as the excuse for it. A densely massed arrangement such as this, relying on flower shapes, colours and textures but no foliage, can be put into a solid and simple basket; in fact the simplicity of such a container will bring the whole extravagant display down to earth and make it homely rather than too formal.

Anchor large pieces of damp florist's foam in the lined basket and tape them in place. You may want to add a layer of crumpled chicken wire over the top if you are using many woody stems or top-heavy flowers which need extra support. Spiky stems of buddleia and antirrhinum have been used to set the limits of height and width so they are positioned first, followed by the other materials used to delineate the edges. Next, add the large globular flowers, such as the big allium heads and the hydrangeas, to the front of the basket. Add a variety of smaller things to fill the space, keeping a smooth surface outline and blending and mixing colours. Aim for the look of a full herbaceous flower border – in this case there is little or no foliage to create contrasts but a mix of light and dark flowers in a small colour range.

Blues, mauves, purples, pinks and burgundies are high summer colours but you could make a similar arrangement using various shades of red or take everything very much paler, using a gentle mixture of soft pinks, creams and whites. Make use of unexpected garden material such as fresh green poppy seed heads or apple mint in flower as useful fillers to cut down on the amount of blooms you would otherwise need. 🌿

LEFT While this mauve and pink arrangement is spectacular and very special it is not formal or too grand, using mostly garden flowers arranged quite simply into a sturdy willow basket.

Haymeadows & Honeysuckle

In early summer roadside verges and hedges are filled with soft grasses and flowering climbers and later there are unripe fruits of wild trees and vines to make use of. Only gather from the wild where you will cause no problems to landowners or the environment. Here, the large wooden trug echoes the look of haymeadows of the past and includes moon daisies amongst flowering grasses, dog roses, elderflowers, sorrel and honeysuckle. High summer also reveals sprays of flowering blackberries, bloomy green sloes, clusters of elderberries and wild clematis.

ABOVE An old French garden trug holds wild hedgerow treasures.
RIGHT A Victorian jug suggests the colour scheme for the wild fruits,
brambles, elderberries, wild plums and clematis inside it.

Summer Blues

Blue is one of the rarer colours in the plant world and all the more prized for that. Beloved of visiting bees, a patch of blue flowers in a summer border is a cool and soothing oasis of colour, imitating the sky above. Blues of all kinds mix well with each other and with mauves and greens. Contrast blue with yellows or apricots or put deep royal blue with reds and purples for a bold, baroque effect. Blue and white is a popular combination too, and always looks fresh, never trite.

There is more choice of blue flowers during the summer than at any other time of year, ranging from the tall columns of delphiniums and campanulas to all the really useful flowers such as scabious, eryngium and echinops. Later there are stately agapanthus and luminous hydrangeas and through the season other annual flowers for picking regularly, such as cornflowers, sweet peas, and the old fashioned convolvulus tricolor. There are many blue annuals which are easily grown from seed and are good for picking so search seed catalogues in winter to make a choice. Blue commonly crosses over into mauve in flowers such as sweet peas and hardy geraniums where a true blue without any hint of pink in it is rare, but all these subtle shades of blue are refreshing to use in summer arrangements.

PREVIOUS PAGE Deepest blues from delphiniums and larkspur.
LEFT Cool pale blues and mauves of a mixed garden bunch look their best displayed in clear glass and are refreshing to the senses.
RIGHT The rich, late summer blues of agapanthus and hydrangea.

59

A Tied Summer Bunch

1

You need hydrangea, vine, sedum, roses, pelargoniums, honeysuckle and polygonum in rich warm reds and bronzes, plus pink silky ribbon for tying the finished bunch and thin wire for securing stems.

2

Prepare all material by trimming stems and removing unwanted leaves. Then, working flat on a surface, position the first layer of vine leaves and hydrangea flower into a spray shape with stems facing towards you.

3

Now begin to add the flowers on top of the background foliage, spreading them out evenly and using smaller blooms at the front and lower down. Tie stems securely in place with wire, but not too tight, to keep a spray shape.

4

Finish by wrapping the ribbon around the stems and over the wire a couple of times, then add a large soft bow. Cut ribbon ends to decorative points and attach a loop of wire to back of the bunch to hang it from a door.

The Timeless Lily

Although we can buy lilies all the year round, they are naturally a summer flower and make a very special addition to any garden. They are often easier to cultivate in pots than taking their chance in a border where they may succumb to bad drainage, insect-carried virus or the wrong soil. As cut flowers they are beautifully long lived with each of the three or more buds on a stem opening out in time. The most fragrant types are *lilium candidum* or the madonna lily, only seen in gardens these days, *lilium longiflorum* with long narrow white trumpets, and the Oriental hybrids such as Casa Blanca with large flowers reflexing to show long stamens. Lilies can be combined successfully with other flowers but look their most striking alone in simple containers. For a very different look, cut flower heads short and float them in shallow water.

ABOVE LEFT Lilies and pelargoniums float in a rich green dish.
ABOVE RIGHT Longiflorum and pink lilies mix well with plain white roses without any fussy extras or foliage in a severe green box.
RIGHT Scented white Casa Blanca lilies and pink spotted Stargazer lilies are simply grouped in tall glass containers.

Garden Vases

Towards the end of the summer the harvesting of garden squashes, pumpkins, melons and gourds should coincide with a last flurry of brightly coloured flowers, such as brilliant nasturtiums, marigolds, cornflowers, poppies and sunflowers. Strong stemmed flowers such as dahlias can be pushed into the flesh of the squash after making a hole for them with a sharp stick or skewer. Two or three flowers in a fruit look best, no more. Flowers which are best bunched together can be put into a reservoir of water made by slicing a thin lid from the top of the squash and scooping out some of the flesh. If you only remove a little flesh the whole container will remain watertight. You may also need to shave a little skin or flesh from the base to make it stand firmly on the ground. Sunflowers are spectacular used in tall arrangements or cut very short and put into low containers alongside some fiery chillies for a very different view of their sun-ray heads.

LEFT Dazzling late summer flowers all in a row with melons and
squashes as colourful containers for crocosmia, dahlias and annuals.
ABOVE Sunflowers make striking, long-lasting cut flowers
whether left naturally tall or cut like these.

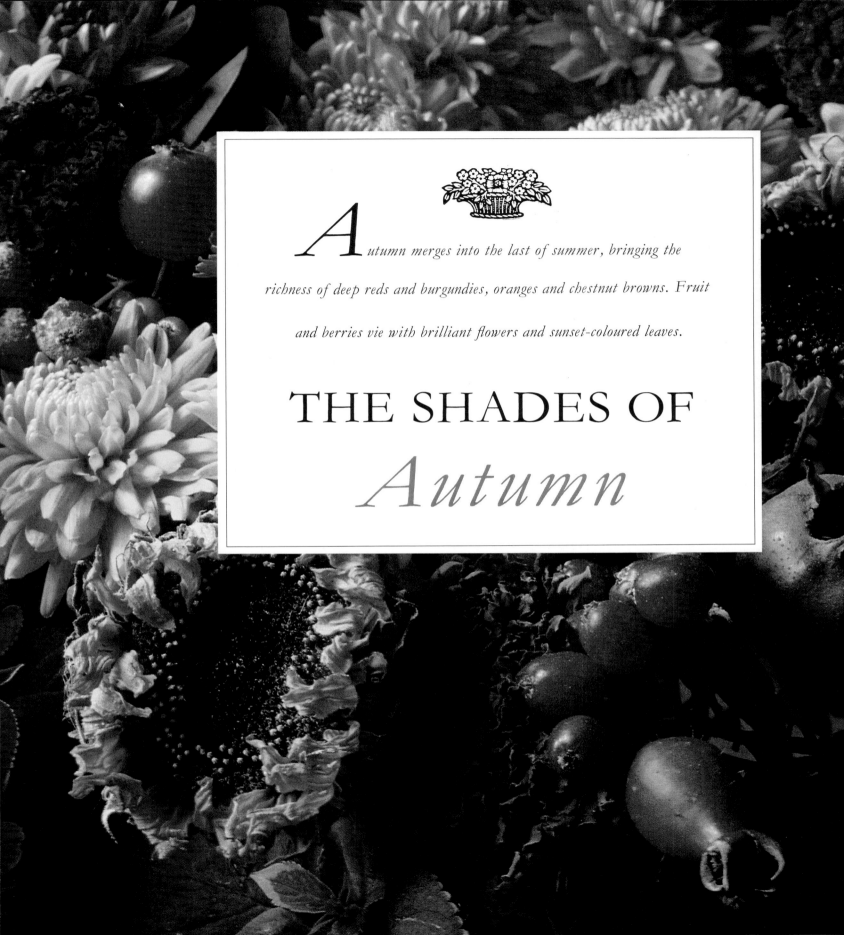

*A*utumn merges into the last of summer, bringing the
richness of deep reds and burgundies, oranges and chestnut browns. Fruit
and berries vie with brilliant flowers and sunset-coloured leaves.

THE SHADES OF
Autumn

Rich Fruits & Brilliant Leaves

Autumn can sometimes be a warm and colourful grand finale to a perfect summer or it can lash the garden with gales and rain or even cut everything short and usher in winter fast with untimely frosts and cold, so what there will be to gather for flower arranging is a slightly unknown quantity. Most years provide fruits, berries and nuts and some marvellous colourful leaves and flowers, other years can see such an abundance of good things that one is spoilt for choice. It makes good sense though to use whatever there is available at this time of year as very soon there will be little to find except expensive, short-lived out-of-season flower shop blooms.

We expect autumn colours to be glowing, fiery and rich, all the shades of orange, gold, flame and red, when in fact there are many more subtle and interesting things to be had, such as the strangely spotted burgundy toad lilies or pale mauve michaelmas daisies. Berries aren't just red and orange either but come in shiny black, deep olive green or blush pink and the earthy shades of brown and ochre appear in nuts, seed pods and

even fruits such as medlars. There are good things to find
in hedgerows and gardens before the clearing up is done in
preparation for winter. Gather colourful leaves to dry and
to press and pick seed heads to preserve or varnish. Twigs
can be bundled together and dried, and different types of
moss collected before the weather gets too unkind. Many berries
will dry to a subtle ghost of their former selves simply by leaving
the stems in a vase of water in a warm place until the fruits
have completely dried out.

Autumn arrangements are by their nature wonderful
mixtures of very different things and dried and fresh material can
be combined without looking at all strange. Simple shapes
and colours seem best for containers for this season's
material to contrast with all the wild twining stems
and rich fruits and berries. Baskets or anything made
from natural materials are another obvious choice
especially when using the stronger autumn colours. Clear
glass and delicate china seems a little too gentle for the very
robust shades and shapes of autumn.

Autumn Monochrome

A monochromatic palette is a welcome change from the strong colours that are unavoidable at this time of year. These understated flowers and fruits include matt white snowberries, glossy black privet, and dogwood fruits and olive green ivy berries which turn black by winter. Combine with glossy evergreen leaves or variegated ivies for contrast. There are white flowers to choose from, such as the suede-textured tuberoses used here in a black and white posy. Their scent is powerful, almost intoxicating, and they last up to two weeks. Another long-lasting white flower is *Ornithogalum arabicum*. The flowers open from the bottom, each with a green central eye. Mixed arrangements of berries, foliage and flowers fade at different rates so change the water frequently and remove dead material.

ABOVE Antique silk bootlaces add style to a monochrome posy.
RIGHT Grouping small collections of things together can make a more
interesting and harmonious finished arrangement.

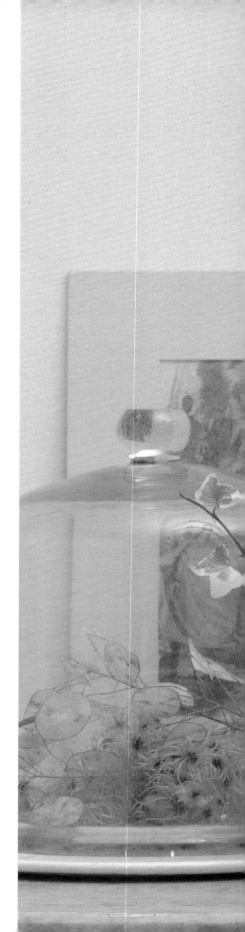

A Feast of Fruits

Berries and fruits are a useful addition to all the other decorative things available during the autumn months. Small fruits can be used as material for arrangements by spearing them onto stiff wires, while larger fruits can be made into decorations by using them as a basis for an arrangement piled into pyramids or carefully balanced into stemmed dishes. Fruits as decorative as pomegranates, quinces or small squashes can be displayed for a few days before eating them, allowing you to enjoy their colours, shapes and scents while they are fleetingly in season. Find your most decorative and unusual dishes and serving plates and simply lay these beautiful specimens out as a feast for the eyes. Tuck a few heads of long-lasting flowers such as chrysanthemums in amongst them or add some richly coloured autumn leaves, fresh or pressed.

Clusters of small bright berries or tiny miniature crab apples look pretty bunched together to make posies or they can be wired round a wreath of any size or shape you like. This is quite a slow process even if you attach small bunches rather than individual berries but the finished result can be left to dry and will look good for many months to come. Pyracantha and cotoneaster shrubs are usually generous with their berries in shades of deep reds and vivid oranges, which can be used to add warmth and colour to all kinds of dried and fresh arrangements.

**LEFT Pomegranates, squashes and tiny yellow
crab apples displayed on Victorian china with a scattering of flowers.
RIGHT Pink peppercorns and pyrancantha berries circle a wreath.**

A Vase of Vegetables

Any fresh materials can work as ingredients for a flower arrangement and vegetables offer unusual shapes, colours and textures. Decorative frilly cabbages and miniature broccoli can be used just like large roses, though you will need to trim off their roots and spike them with a wooden skewer to hold them in place. Use a foam base and wire netting inside the container. Secure smaller items in the foam with a stiff wire pushed into the bottom of the vegetable and them into the foam. Leave turnips in the light for a few days to sprout tufts of fresh green foliage.

ABOVE Trails of ivy and amaranthus add a finishing touch.
RIGHT Homely Brussels sprouts and turnips assume a glamorous role
when combined with asparagus, broccoli and frilly cabbages.

A Harvest Bundle

1

Glue bottom part of wheat and rye stems to a black plastic flower pot, ideally using an electric glue gun. The stems should come a little way above the top of the pot. Cut a block of florist's foam to fit snugly inside the pot and push neatly into place.

2

Once you have glued stems around the pot, put an elastic band round it and begin to tuck the top part of wheat and rye stems behind the band to make a full stook effect. Cut stems to make them roughly the same length. Cut three strands of string to tie around the pot.

3

Knot the string and remove rubber band. Add dried flowers to make a solid texture inside the stook. Put small flowers such as roses into groups to give good blocks of colour. Here there are dried sunflowers, yellow roses, echinops, red zinnias and dark grey poppy seed heads inside the wheat and rye.

Clashing Colours

Autumn colours can be surprising. The sharp, shocking pink of nerines seems to come from a different season but they bloom in the garden through late autumn into the winter, as so do *Schizostylis*, another flowering bulb sometimes known as Kaffir Lily, which comes in varying shades of red, pink and coral. These useful flowers offer material for cutting when there is beginning to be a shortage of it, apart from the stalwarts such as Michaelmas daisies and chrysanthemums. Try mixing these clear, shocking pink flowers with the brilliant flames and oranges of autumn berries for an invigorating arrangement.

Berries of all kinds are plentiful right through the autumn and many such as rose hips are tough enough to last well into winter before the birds eventually strip the branches. Pyracantha, viburnum, dogwood, euonymus and cotoneaster are just a few of the shrubs providing berries. There are more delicate kinds too, like the multi-coloured green through yellow and orange to red of wild bryony which twines it way through hedgerows and shines out in late autumn amongst the bare brown branches of its hosts.

For such a bold mixture of clashing colours, the container you choose should be as plain and simple as possible with a strong and definite shape. This large arrangement is made from nerines combined with deep purplish-pink Michaelmas daisies, some from the garden and some from the flower shop, in equal quantities. The arching stems of *euphorbia fulgens* arranged amongst these add movement and spots of brilliant colour. The small leaves which grow along the whole stem of the euphorbia have been taken off which has the effect of making the colour of the flowers more intense (these are actually coloured bracts not petals).

PREVIOUS PAGE Strings of autumn leaves, fruits
and berries show the variety and subtlety of the season's harvest.

LEFT A daring colour scheme can work if you are not fainthearted even
when it comes to a background for the arrangement.

Fallen Leaves

For a few short magical days in autumn the colour of the leaves in gardens and countryside can reach a spectacular crescendo of reds, golds and oranges. There are subtler colours, too, in vine leaves, shrubs and plants with hitherto quite unremarkable colouring. Leaves of all shapes and textures can be used fresh, or dried and pressed flat, to add to arrangements with flowers and berries or to wrap containers, make mats to stand pots on or to use as decorative motifs to attach to whatever you fancy, whether it is a shelf edge or a picture frame. Make use of the marvellous textures and surface detail of leaves and any which you press will be dry enough to keep and use for many more months to come. The easiest way to press leaves is in single layers between newspaper under a heavy weight.

ABOVE LEFT **Fresh vine leaves wrap a pot filled with aubergines and hydrangeas. Bright green string adds just the right colour note.**
ABOVE RIGHT **Pressed leaves layered under plates show off ripe figs.**
RIGHT **Rings of dried eucalyptus leaves decorate shelves filled with arrangements of fresh and pressed vine and prunus leaves.**

A Flower for Michaelmas

Michaelmas daisies are the very essence of the autumn garden with their misty colours and soft, starry clouds of flowers. Tough and long-lived, they are often taken for granted at this time of year but appear to be making a comeback in gardens. With the introduction of new, mildew-resistant varieties, they seem to have become suddenly fashionable again. Equally at home in a crowded cottage garden or elegant herbaceous border, they also make marvellous cut flowers as they last and last in water. Their shape and structure makes them more of a filler in grand arrangements rather than important star material but in more homely and countrified decorations they quickly and easily fill a jug or basket and more or less do the arranging for you.

Flower shops sell a choice of varieties through much of the year now and the colour range is normally from pale mauve to deep purple plus a milky white version. The little starry flowers vary in size from tiny single ones with small centres to larger, multi-petalled types with striking golden eyes. Use them as long-stemmed as possible for large scale displays or cut short pieces from a bunch to use in smaller, more delicate posies and miniature arrangements. Michaelmas daisies mix well with all kinds of other autumnal material and look good with simple, strong-shaped flowers or foliage to contrast with their soft, fuzzy outlines.

In the arrangement here, a pale mauve garden-grown daisy is mixed with a deeper purple variety, with a few branches of elder added to give a wonderful contrast in colour and shape. The elder leaves are almost ready to fall and have reached a pretty, pale, almost washed out yellow with just a hint of pink veining. Such a large scale arrangement would look splendid in a hall, in the centre of a living room table or even standing at floor level or in a fireplace.

LEFT An unusual French fifties metal jug in Parma violet makes the right
solid base for a cloud of frothy Michaelmas daisies, with the yellow
leaves separating the different shades of mauve and purple.

Twigs & Stems

While coloured leaves are a symbol of autumn and the dramatic change of season, the first bare twigs are a reminder of the bleaker winter season to come. Twigs used with fresh flowers, berries and foliage make excellent decorations and you can use garden prunings as raw material or buy bundles of twigs from flower shops. Twigs don't have to be brown or grey – plants such as willow and cornus have brightly coloured stems in reds, oranges and yellows. 🍂

ABOVE **Birth twigs glued to a container hold sunny chrysanthemums.**
RIGHT **Low autumn sun highlights twisted and golden willow stems in an
orange vase wrapped round with a circlet of berried bryony vine.**

Autumn Choices

Autumn offers a very wide range of materials to use in arrangements, from seed pods and nuts, mosses and fruits, to leaves, berries and many different flowers. The way to approach using them all is simply to treat the material as you would any ordinary flowers and foliage; very few will need special treatment. Small things such as nuts may need to be glued to a stem made of wood or stiff wire. Wooden food skewers are good for this purpose and can also be used for fruits which can be speared easily and then added to an arrangement. Some seed heads such as clematis with their light fluffy strands may need to be sprayed with a fixative or varnish of some kind to hold them together. A few other ingredients can also benefit from this treatment, *iris foetidissima* pods in particular, otherwise the berries fall out as they open up and dry.

Most berried branches will last well in water as many have to remain like this in the wild with leafless stems for months until the fruits are eaten by birds and the seed distributed. Coloured autumn leaves on trees and shrubs are a little trickier to handle as the leaves are often on the point of dropping when their colours are at their most brilliant and useable. Treat them gently when getting them home, then once they are in an arrangement their leaves may drop gradually over a few days. A mist of hairspray or fixative may help, aimed where the leaf stem joins the branch.

Containers for autumn ingredients can be really rustic and countrified so baskets and wooden containers of all types work well. Here a collection of pale, split wood baskets and boxes are linked by their soft texture and colour and look just right with the rich brown papery oak leaves and brilliant *physalis* lanterns. Line baskets and boxes with plastic to make them waterproof or stand a container inside.

LEFT A group of containers each holding mixtures of different autumnal ingredients. Some have one type only and most no more than three combined. This makes for a strong and simple look instead of a chaotic muddle.

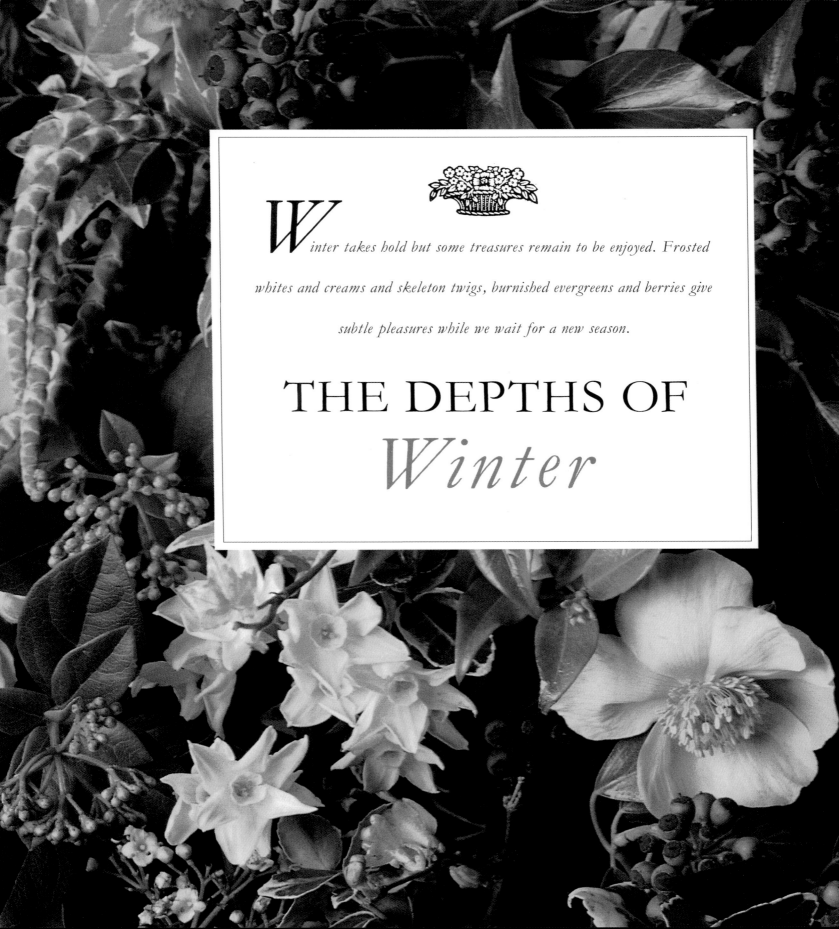

W

inter takes hold but some treasures remain to be enjoyed. Frosted whites and creams and skeleton twigs, burnished evergreens and berries give subtle pleasures while we wait for a new season.

THE DEPTHS OF
Winter

Fragrant Flowers & Frosted Twigs

Winter need not be a barren time for fresh flowers as many spring flowers and bulbs are grown under protection or flown in from warmer places for sale well before their normal outdoor harvesting. It always seems a little strange, though, to fill the house with daffodils even before Christmas has been and gone. It is also becoming increasingly possible to buy summer flowers throughout the year, rather like the ever-present strawberry in the supermarket. The drawback is that these flowers are often expensive and don't always last well. Flowering plants and bulbs seem better value somehow, with many such as azaleas and cyclamen providing flowers over several years with a little care, providing you have the space and conditions to keep them. Amaryllis bulbs make spectacular and long-lasting decorations and traditionally bowls of paper-white narcissi were always grown for Christmas. They can be planted in late autumn in pebbles or soil and will flower in just a few weeks. Look out for pots of winter-flowering pansies and early primroses, often sold for planting into gardens and containers, but equally happy for a short time indoors.

Winter decorations need not concentrate on flowers either, as there are all kinds of stems and twigs and good evergreen foliage which can be used to make arrangements. The winter garden may seem bleak and bare but search carefully and you may find a few scented flowering branches or a late, late rose, winter iris, or berries left by the birds. Any offering at this time of year is welcome and valuable,

and if you have to think miniature rather than grand scale in your arrangements then why not do so for a few weeks before there is plenty to choose from again.

If you do have a garden then consider planting a few special things just for winter picking for the house even if you have space for only a basic but useful shrub such as *viburnum tinus* which should keep you in good green foliage and sprays of pinkish white flowers for weeks on end.

Many of the winter-flowering garden plants compensate for their delicate and subtle flowers with powerful scents much prized during winter months. The delicious fresh citrus or honey fragrance of flowers such as mahonia or wintersweet make them very special plants indeed. You only need to pick a small piece of flowering branch or a sprig or two of something scented to make an instant decoration for a table or mantel shelf or to put under a pool of lamp light to cheer a long winter night. Winter flowers have their own subtle but quite compelling kind of charm so explore gardens and hedgerows to seek out these treasures.

Subtlety & Scent

Paradoxically, in the midst of winter the garden offers some of the most beautiful, delicate and perfumed flowers of the year, including miniature iris in shades of mauve and purple and deep yellow which last well as cut flowers. Choose the smallest liqueur glasses to display them in and enjoy the blooms indoors, safe from frosts, drenching rain or greedy snails. Many winter-flowering shrubs have the most sweetly scented blossoms flowering on their bare stems. Just a sprig or two of *chimonanthus fragrans* (wintersweet), *lonicera purpusii* (winter honeysuckle) or *mahonia japonica* will fill the room with fragrance. There are other colourful treasures to be found too, such as cyclamen, winter jasmine and tiny winter-flowering crocus, all more precious than many a large and showy summer flower. Display all these winter finds simply in small glasses where their shapes are defined and seen clearly.

ABOVE Miniature iris and crocus hint at a spring to come.
RIGHT The winter garden's subtle offerings displayed in simple
containers are more special than summer's largesse.

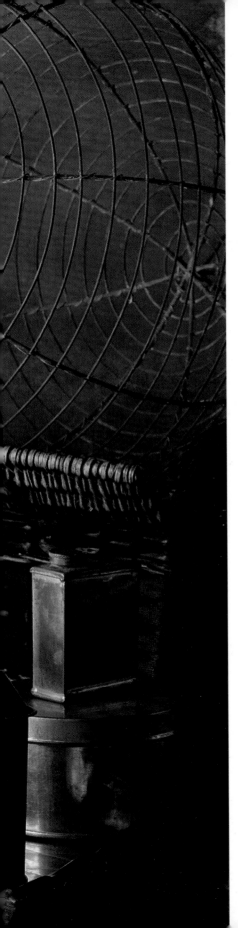

Winter Pansies

Winter pansies are widely grown and sold as outdoor plants to fill tubs and containers in the garden during the winter months. They make excellent short-term plants for indoor too, and once you have enjoyed their flowers for a while the plants can be put out into the garden to take their chance and perhaps flower again. Pansies have a wide-eyed kind of innocence and charm which is hard to resist. Plants like these are best put singly into suitable containers or several massed into one larger pot. They don't look nearly as good mixed with other kinds of plants. Beware of some of the pansies sold with enormously heavy, oversized flower heads on short stems. These many look fine as a massed bedding scheme in a park, but have lost the essential style of the pansy. Look for smaller flowers, closer to a viola, on longish stems. Colours are wonderful – deep velvet purple and blue, burgundy, burnt orange, yellow and white.

Choose robust-looking containers made from terracotta or metal. Glass or delicate china do not seem appropriate and whatever you choose must be suitable to contain the soil-filled pot in which the pansy is growing. Here the lustre of old pewter and burnished tin throws up the richness of colour and texture of the pansy blooms. Single colours or shades look better than many different ones together.

LEFT Four small pansy plants in varying shades of purple have a temporary indoor home in a deep pewter bowl. ABOVE Single pansies look striking in a metal pail.

Pink & Silver

We rather take for granted plants such as cyclamen which are so commonly available during the winter months but they are good value, providing brilliant colour for several weeks. The smaller flowered types are very often prettier than the larger varieties and their pot size means that they can be slipped into all kinds of interesting outer containers. Bright, shiny metal tins and kitchen moulds make sparkling and festive places for a pink or red-flowered plant or two. Use a little moss to cover the soil inside the container. This colour scheme of silver and pink is unusual but just as festive as traditional red and green.

PREVIOUS PAGE **Christmas decorations in natural ingredients and taffeta.**
LEFT **Garden and pot plant cyclamen blooms in a mercury glass container.**
ABOVE **Silver and pink provide an unusual twist to the festive theme.**

A Gilded Frame

1

You will need an electric glue gun, bronze
powder and paint medium, nuts, dried seed
heads, artichoke heads and large leaves such
as magnolia. Use long twigs of cinnamon or
other wood for the frame.

2

Mix bronze powder with paint medium in a
small container and paint, using a small brush,
on to the leaves, nuts and seeds but not twigs.
Leave to dry thoroughly before beginning to
assemble the frame.

3

Glue four straight cinnamon sticks together to
form basis of frame. Add some smaller twigs
to the frame to make it thicker. Paint the frame
with gold paint and leave to dry. Plan where to
glue the gilded decorations on the frame.

4

Glue the largest things, such as the artichokes,
on first, then fill in with small nuts and seeds.
Either leave the frame flat at the back to hang
on a wall or glue on supports so it can stand to
frame an arrangement or evergreen topiary.

Candle Power

The effect of candlelight and flowers together is heady and glamorous but at the same time warm and welcoming. Candlelight can subtly change colours from their daylight version to something much more mellow, so bear this in mind when choosing colour schemes and opt for pale pastels which can afford to be warmed up by the golden glow from fat cream candles.

When winter flowers are scarce and expensive, combine fresh with dried or mix real and artificial blooms together. In these kind of festive decorations what does it matter which are used to create the right effect? Add touches of sparkle and glitter with a few gilded leaves or gold or silver Christmas baubles in amongst a cream and white flower decoration. Group several church candles together, fixing them securely to the base of a round, shallow glass dish with foam or special candle supports. Around this build a circle of pale dried hydrangeas and place a few stems of something exotic, such as white amaryllis, in more foam. Small, gold, glass balls on wires pushed in at random throughout the flowers complete the decoration.

Decorate single cream candles with small foam rings covered with dried hydrangea in pale pistachio green and soft pink interspersed with freeze-dried creamy pink roses which look as real as the fresh summer version. Gluing the flowers into place is the easiest and most secure method. Use only slow-burning candles and never leave them alight in a room without people around to keep watch if they burn down low near the flowers.

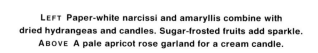

LEFT **Paper-white narcissi and amaryllis combine with dried hydrangeas and candles. Sugar-frosted fruits add sparkle.**
ABOVE **A pale apricot rose garland for a cream candle.**

Frosted Whites

Few flowers sum up winter more precisely than snowdrops and Christmas roses (*helleborus niger*). Hellebores can be difficult to get to flower at the right time, often needing protection from slugs, snails and winter mud splashes to keep them pristine. Many other hellebore hybrids are easier to grow and just as beautiful. Snowdrops are simple and if you don't grow them, most flower shops sell them in irresistible miniature bunches. They need nothing more than a sprig or two of ivy or an evergreen leaf mixed with them. Display them in small vases — white china is ideal — and enjoy their green and white innocence and delicacy. Several snowdrop-filled small containers can look more effective than a mass of flowers crowded into one larger bowl.

ABOVE **Snowdrops look their best in small groups.**
RIGHT **Winter-flowering hellebores ranging from cream to palest lime green in an old Leedsware bowl.**

Glorious Reds

Red is a colour that we might not choose for flowers in other seasons but in winter it seems entirely right. Strong and cheering, it looks good in grey daylight, pale winter sunshine or warm artificial light at night. It is associated with Christmas traditions and is generally combined with dark greens, but used alone or with just the minimum of colour contrast it glows magically and lifts the spirits.

Many winter flowers look best used very simply and not combined with other materials. A strong concentrated blast of colour is more welcome than a diluted fussy mixture. The red of anemones is pure and bright, enhanced by the inky black centres of each bloom. Every flower has its little tangled ruff of green behind the petals which is enough to separate the blooms and provide a neat colour contrast. The velvet texture of anemones is best complemented by pewter, shiny silver or any metal, dark polished wood, or china with a deep coloured glaze. Avoid pale colours or clear glass, though cobalt blue or ruby glass would look beautiful with matching flowers. Italian-grown long-stemmed anemones are sold in bunches of single colours and last for many days.

Equally rich in colour, but with a more exotic look to them, are amaryllis or hippeastrum. Their origins are tropical but they have become known as winter-flowering bulbs in northern countires, sold either as cut flowers or as growing plants. Red Lion is a good, red cut flower variety with dusty golden stamens and flower heads held at right angles to the hollow stems. It may seem a shame to cut down these stems, but once shortened the flowers are much more useful and manageable for many flower arrangments. Two or three stems of amaryllis are enough to fill a medium jug or vase and last for two weeks. Remove flower heads as they die and the buds further up the stem will open to take their place.

RIGHT **Red amaryllis alone in a silver lustre glazed jug, anemones in a silver cornucopia vase and the two combined in a mistletoe-patterned jug make a glowing winter still life.**

A Moss Harvest

Moss of all kinds has great creative possibilities. Gather your own from the garden or buy from a reliable source; never plunder the countryside. All kinds of flowers look good set off by this green texture. Small pieces of velvet bun moss pushed into tiny containers make a lovely background for displaying single blooms or try a long row of flowers equally spaced along a narrow dish. Use flat moss to cover the base of growing bulbs or tuck it in at the bottom of any arrangement, especially baskets, to conceal ugly stems or floral foam. Wrap large sheets of flat moss around vases and containers, holding it in place with thin reel wire which merges into the moss and doesn't show. Spray moss regularly with water to hold its fresh green colour or leave it to dry out slowly and naturally. It retains plenty of colour even when fully dry.

LEFT Simple, shapely glass vases wrapped in fresh moss.
ABOVE LEFT   A collection of cut glass salt cellars tightly
filled with bright green bun moss displaying single winter blooms.
ABOVE RIGHT Moss-wrapped spheres and hyacinth bulbs.

INDEX